Wildebeest Migration

by Kari Schuetz

BLASTOFF! READERS
3

BELLWETHER MEDIA • MINNEAPOLIS, MN

Note to Librarians, Teachers, and Parents:

Blastoff! Readers are carefully developed by literacy experts and combine standards-based content with developmentally appropriate text.

Level 1 provides the most support through repetition of high-frequency words, light text, predictable sentence patterns, and strong visual support.

Level 2 offers early readers a bit more challenge through varied simple sentences, increased text load, and less repetition of high-frequency words.

Level 3 advances early-fluent readers toward fluency through increased text and concept load, less reliance on visuals, longer sentences, and more literary language.

Level 4 builds reading stamina by providing more text per page, increased use of punctuation, greater variation in sentence patterns, and increasingly challenging vocabulary.

Level 5 encourages children to move from "learning to read" to "reading to learn" by providing even more text, varied writing styles, and less familiar topics.

Whichever book is right for your reader, Blastoff! Readers are the perfect books to build confidence and encourage a love of reading that will last a lifetime!

This edition first published in 2019 by Bellwether Media, Inc.

No part of this publication may be reproduced in whole or in part without written permission of the publisher. For information regarding permission, write to Bellwether Media, Inc., Attention: Permissions Department, 6012 Blue Circle Drive, Minnetonka, MN 55343.

Library of Congress Cataloging-in-Publication Data

Names: Schuetz, Kari, author.
Title: Wildebeest Migration / by Kari Schuetz.
Description: Minneapolis, MN : Bellwether Media, Inc., 2019. | Series:
   Blastoff! Readers. Animals on the Move | Audience: Age 5-8. | Audience:
   Grade K to 3. | Includes bibliographical references and index.
Identifiers: LCCN 2018000196 (print) | LCCN 2018005327 (ebook) | ISBN
   9781626178205 (hardcover : alk. paper) | ISBN 9781681035611 (ebook)
Subjects: LCSH: Gnus--Migration--Juvenile literature.
Classification: LCC QL737.U53 (ebook) | LCC QL737.U53 S325 2019 (print) | DDC 599.64/591568--dc23
LC record available at https://lccn.loc.gov/2018000196

Editor: Paige V. Polinsky   Designer: Jeffrey Kollock

Printed in the United States of America, North Mankato, MN

Table of Contents

Wildebeest

Wildebeest are **nomads** that wander grassy **plains**. These **mammals** must travel far for food and water.

Wildebeest Profile

animal type: **mammal**

habitats: **grassy plains, open woodlands**

size: **height at shoulder: 4.5 feet (1.4 meters)**
weight: up to 600 pounds (272 kilograms)

life span: **about 20 years**

Every year, the largest **herds** circle eastern Africa. Their group **migration** includes more than one million travelers!

Wildebeest have long legs and strong **hooves** for safe roaming. They can **sprint** away from **predators** or run them over.

sprinting

hooves

Their hooves also leave **scent trails** behind. Lost wildebeest can follow these to find their herd.

To Greener Grasses

As the **dry season** approaches, wildebeest leave their southern **range**.

Adults and young **calves** must move from place to place to **graze**. Their hunger and thirst will take them in a loop.

calf

East African Wildebeest Departure

mode of travel: walking

leaving
April: Serengeti National Park

arriving
July: Masai Mara National Reserve

Separate herds of wildebeest set out slowly in the same direction. They all head north.

herd

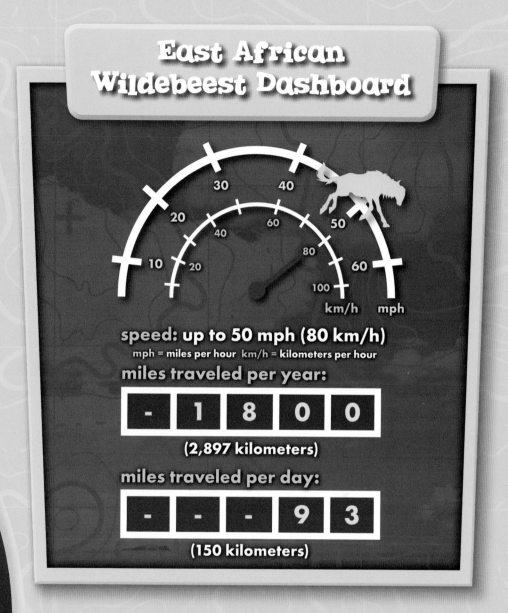

East African Wildebeest Dashboard

speed: up to 50 mph (80 km/h)

mph = miles per hour km/h = kilometers per hour

miles traveled per year:

| - | 1 | 8 | 0 | 0 |

(2,897 kilometers)

miles traveled per day:

| - | - | - | 9 | 3 |

(150 kilometers)

Many zebras and gazelles join them. Traveling as a group is much safer than traveling alone.

Making the Loop

watering hole

Rain directs when and where wildebeest move. Fresh plants and **watering holes** guide their way.

Lions, cheetahs, and hyenas speed the herd along at times. These predators chase to attack.

cheetah

Africa

N
W   E
S

Rut slows the trip north.
This is when male wildebeest
stop traveling to compete.

East African Wildebeest Migration

Lake Victoria

Kenya
Tanzania

river
Serengeti
Masai Mara
departure trip (April–July)
return trip (October–January)

N
W   E
S

0   25
miles

Each male claims a space to guard. There, he only welcomes females. The wildebeest continue their journey after a few weeks.

Wildebeest herds face great danger when they cross rivers. Many drown in the deep water.

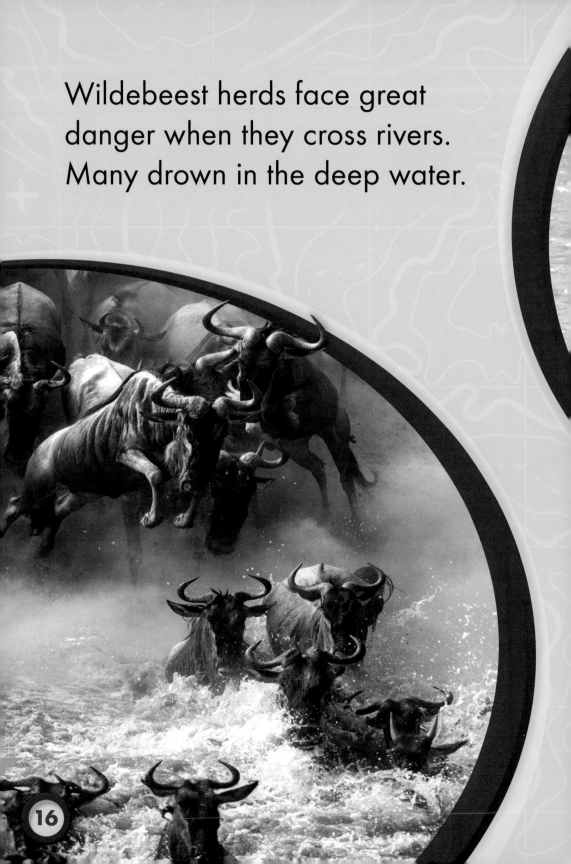

crocodile

Hungry crocodiles also wait there to attack. They make some wildebeest into meals.

Born to Roam

Wildebeest roam their northern range for months. They later follow the wet weather back south.

Females give birth to calves there in February. As many as 500,000 calves are born in two weeks!

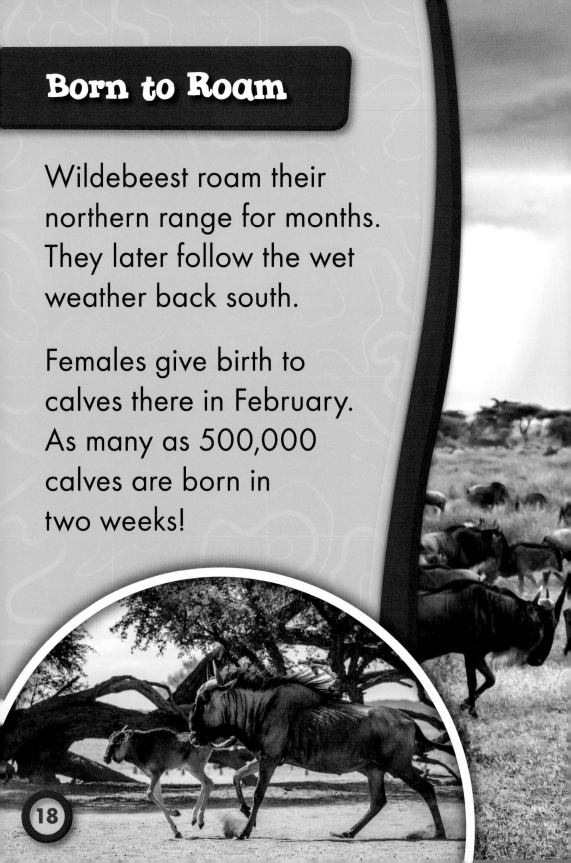

East African Wildebeest Return

mode of travel: walking

leaving
October: Masai Mara National Reserve

arriving
January: Serengeti National Park

Newborn calves are natural travelers. They can stand and walk almost right away. Their survival depends on escaping predators.

The baby wildebeest must also keep up with the adults. Their first migration begins in just months!

Glossary

calves—baby wildebeest

dry season—a time of year when it rains very little

graze—to feed on grasses

herds—groups of wildebeest

hooves—hard coverings on the feet of wildebeest

mammals—warm-blooded animals that have backbones and feed their young milk

migration—the act of traveling from one place to another, often with the seasons

nomads—travelers that roam from place to place

plains—large areas of flat lands

predators—animals that hunt other animals for food

range—the area where an animal can be found

rut—when male wildebeest compete for land and females

scent trails—smells left by wildebeest that mark the migration path

sprint—to run at full speed for a short distance

watering holes—pools of water from which animals drink

To Learn More

AT THE LIBRARY
Davies, Monika. *How Far Home? Animal Migrations.* Mankato, Minn.: Amicus Illustrated, 2019.

Fishman, Jon M. *The Wildebeest's Journey.* Minneapolis, Minn.: Lerner Publications, 2018.

Hansen, Grace. *Wildebeest Migration.* Minneapolis, Minn.: ABDO Kids, 2018.

ON THE WEB
Learning more about wildebeest migration is as easy as 1, 2, 3.

1. Go to www.factsurfer.com.

2. Enter "wildebeest migration" into the search box.

3. Click the "Surf" button and you will see a list of related web sites.

With factsurfer.com, finding more information is just a click away.

Index

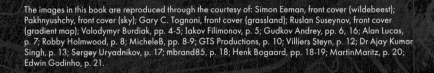

The images in this book are reproduced through the courtesy of: Simon Eeman, front cover (wildebeest); Pakhnyushchy, front cover (sky); Gary C. Tognoni, front cover (grassland); Ruslan Suseynov, front cover (gradient map); Volodymyr Burdiak, pp. 4-5; Iakov Filimonov, p. 5; Gudkov Andrey, pp. 6, 16; Alan Lucas, p. 7; Robby Holmwood, p. 8; MicheleB, pp. 8-9; GTS Productions, p. 10; Villiers Steyn, p. 12; Dr Ajay Kumar Singh, p. 13; Sergey Uryadnikov, p. 17; mbrand85, p. 18; Henk Bogaard, pp. 18-19; MartinMaritz, p. 20; Edwin Godinho, p. 21.